WHAT ARE COMMUNITY SERVICES?

LISA IDZIKOWSKI

Britannica
Educational Publishing

IN ASSOCIATION WITH

ROSEN
EDUCATIONAL SERVICES

Published in 2018 by Britannica Educational Publishing (a trademark of Encyclopædia Britannica, Inc.) in association with The Rosen Publishing Group, Inc., 29 East 21st Street, New York, NY 10010.

Distributed exclusively by Rosen Publishing.
To see additional Britannica Educational Publishing titles, go to rosenpublishing.com.

First Edition

Britannica Educational Publishing
J.E. Luebering: Executive Director, Core Editorial
Mary Rose McCudden: Editor, Britannica Student Encyclopedia

Rosen Publishing
Heather Moore Niver: Editor
Nelson Sá: Art Director
Matt Cauli: Designer
Ellina Litmanovich: Book Layout
Cindy Reiman: Photography Manager
Heather Moore Niver: Photo Researcher

Library of Congress Cataloging-in-Publication Data

Names: Idzikowski, Lisa, author.
Title: What are community services? / Lisa Idzikowski.
Description: First edition. | New York, NY : Britannica Educational Publishing, 2018. | Series: Let's find out! Communities | Includes bibliographical references and index.
Identifiers: LCCN 2016058550| ISBN 9781680487275 (library bound : alk. paper) | ISBN 9781680487251 pbk. : alk. paper) | ISBN 9781680487268 (6-pack : alk. paper)
Subjects: LCSH: Community life—Juvenile literature. | Human services—Juvenile literature. | Municipal services—Juvenile literature. | Communities—Juvenile literature.
Classification: LCC HM761 .I39 2018 | DDC 307—dc23
LC record available at https://lccn.loc.gov/2016058550

Manufactured in the United States of America

Photo credits: Cover, p. 1, interior pages (background) John De Bord/Shutterstock.com; p. 4 bowdenimages/iStock/Thinkstock; p. 5 LuckyBusiness/iStock/Thinkstock; p. 6 XiXinXing/Thinkstock; p. 7 monkeybusinessimages/iStock/Thinkstock; p. 8 aijohn784/iStock/Thinkstock; p. 9 Trinette Reed/Blend Images/Thinkstock; p. 10 shironosov/iStock/Thinkstock; p. 11 Nick White/DigitalVision/Thinkstock; p. 12 Comstock Images/Stockbyte/Thinkstock; p. 13 DragonImages/iStock/Thinkstock; p. 14 spwidoff/Shutterstock.com; p. 15 Khosro/Shutterstock.com; p. 16 ChainFoto24/Shutterstock.com; pp. 17, 20 moodboard/Thinkstock; p. 18 Pierre Desrosiers/iStock/Thinkstock; p. 19 Nejron Photo/Shutterstock.com; p. 21 AndreyPopov/iStock/Thinkstock; p. 22 Andersen Ross/Blend Images/Thinkstock; p. 23 xalanx/iStock/Thinkstock; p. 24 ChiccoDodiFC/Shutterstock.com; p. 25 RichLegg/iStock/Thinkstock; p. 26 Dangubic/iStock/Thinkstock; p. 27 Blur Life 1975/Shutterstock.com; p. 28 mari_art/iStock/Thinkstock; p. 29 Rob Marmion/Hemera/Thinkstock.

CONTENTS

Community Services All Around

A community is a place where people live, work, play, and help each other. A community, whether large or small, also provides services to meet the needs and wants of its members.

Needs are what people must have in order to survive: a place to live, food to eat, and water to drink. Wants are things that people would like to have but that are

People of all ages live, work, play, and help each other in their communities.

4

not necessary for survival, such as a new bike or car. Goods and services satisfy people's wants and needs.

Goods include such objects as apples, cars, and roads. Services are things that people do for others. Gymnastics lessons, banking, and dental care are all services.

Take a walk, pedal a bike, or ride in a car to explore a nearby community. Businesses, play areas, shops, and workers are ready to supply all kinds of community services.

Dental care is just one of many kinds of services provided in most communities.

COMPARE AND CONTRAST

What is the difference between a good and a service? List five goods and five services found in your community.

Look Closely at Your Community

Communities come in every size. Urban communities are large cities with many people, buildings, and businesses. Areas called suburbs lie outside the boundaries of cities. Many people live in the suburbs and commute, or travel, to their jobs in the city. Rural communities are small and out in the country away from cities or suburbs.

Communities have two kinds of services available to their citizens: private and public. Private services are those

People often use public transportation when commuting to their jobs in the city.

The services that firefighters provide help keep communities safe.

that individuals provide. People pay money directly to businesses for private services, such as a stylist cutting hair or a veterinarian caring for a sick pet. Public services are provided by the community. The members of the community pay for the services through taxes, or money that the members pay to the community. Common public services include protection by police and fire departments, road building, and public education.

THINK ABOUT IT

Why are public services available to everyone in a community? What kinds of services are those?

Safety and Savings Are Their Business

Car accidents, crime, fires, and health problems happen everywhere. However, people trust that their police, fire, and ambulance services are ready to help. Families feel secure because of community safety services.

People who work earn an income. Workers deposit their money in bank accounts at banks and credit

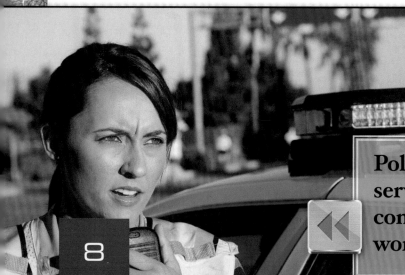

Police officers protect and serve the neighborhoods and communities where they work.

8

People pay monthly bills for some goods and services their families use regularly, such as heating and electricity.

unions. Most people have a checking account, so they can write checks to pay for goods and services for their family. Some people also keep money in savings accounts to earn interest. Interest is money that the bank pays for every dollar that someone has in their savings account.

Some people borrow money from banks. Loans help them buy expensive items like homes or cars. People pay the loan back in monthly portions called installments. If the borrower does not repay, the bank may take away the thing (a car, for example) that the loan was used to buy.

VOCABULARY

People receive money for the work they do. This money is called an **income.**

TIME TO LEARN

What do schools, libraries, and museums have in common? Community members of all ages can learn about math, mice, moths, and more at these places of learning and discovery. Teachers, librarians, and museum curators work to educate others at these institutions.

Schools are places where children go to learn. Every school serves the same purpose: to educate students.

A library has books, newspapers, magazines, films, audio recordings, and computer software. Most public libraries have

Teachers have an important job. They work to educate all the students in their classrooms.

computers that people can use for free. Librarians keep the resources in order. They show people how to find and use them.

Museums inspire interest and understanding by displaying objects from many different times and places. They may also offer services such as guided tours, lectures, and special events. Scientists and other scholars sometimes use museums to do research. Want to learn about art, history, science, or even baseball? Visit a museum!

THINK ABOUT IT

What is something you can do at a museum that you cannot do in your classroom?

Museums encourage community members to observe and learn about all sorts of interesting things.

Health Care for You and Your Pet

Illnesses and injuries happen to every member of a community. People sprain their ankles, catch colds, and get toothaches. Their pets get fleas and hurt their paws. In a community, citizens have places to go to receive medical care.

People want to be healthy, so they count on others to provide medical services. Someone with a serious injury goes to the hospital emergency room for treatment. Parents take sick children to see the doctor at an office or clinic. Someone with a sore tooth

Veterinarians are specialists who provide medical services for all kinds of animals in the community.

Many children go to the doctor for a check-up or when they are sick. Pediatricians are doctors who care for children.

makes a dental appointment. Pet owners hurry their wounded dog to the veterinarian.

Doctors are people with many years of education and training. They are skilled specialists who help keep people healthy and heal the sick. Dentists, nurses, veterinarians, and other health care workers are also highly skilled. In a community, everyone depends on these workers to provide health care services for people and animals.

VOCABULARY

A **specialist** is a person who does a specific job within a broader field. For example, a pediatrician is a doctor who provides health care to children.

13

COMMUNITY CLEANLINESS

Several services help communities enjoy clean streets and safe drinking water. Recycling centers, garbage pick-up, and water treatment plants help keep communities clean and also protect their natural resources.

Many materials—aluminum cans, glass bottles, newspapers, magazines, and plastics—can be recycled. Recycling reuses materials instead of throwing them away to pollute the land, air, and water. In some communities, recycling and garbage pick-up are private services. In others, the services are provided by the community.

Communities often offer recycling services for cans, plastic, paper, and other materials.

Communities usually operate systems to provide clean, safe drinking water.

Members of the community receive the services because they pay taxes to the community.

In some areas, people get their water straight from a river or a well. Large cities and towns, however, have public systems that provide water to their residents and businesses. Water supply systems usually collect, clean, store, and distribute water.

BUILDING AND FIXING THINGS

As communities grow, they need to build new houses, schools, offices, and stores. They also need to build and repair freeways, roads, and bridges. These structures help keep communities operating. Construction workers perform all of this work. Many different kinds of workers may be involved in a construction project. Some have particular skills. Electricians, plumbers, roofers, and carpenters are all special types of workers.

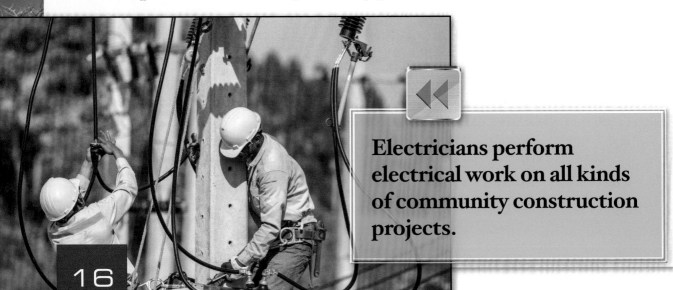

Electricians perform electrical work on all kinds of community construction projects.

◀◀

Construction workers use blueprints while building all sorts of projects for the community.

Construction workers may be hired by a city to work on public projects or they may be hired by individuals. For example, potholes make the streets bumpy and difficult to drive on. City workers fill and fix potholes to make the road smooth again. If the lights are not working in your house, your parents might hire an electrician to come fix them.

THINK ABOUT IT

What would happen if there were no city workers to fix the streets and buildings in a community?

GETTING AROUND TOWN

People move around town in many different ways. They may walk to school or the playground, bicycle to the park, drive a car to work, or ride a bus to the mall. People also use transportation to move goods from one place to another. When crops are ready, farmers box and send them to market. Sometimes, this is a small, local market where people from the area come to buy fresh food. Other times, the food

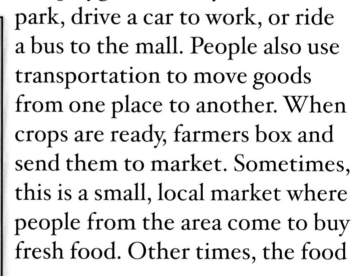

Baskets of delicious ripe tomatoes are ready to be transported to market.

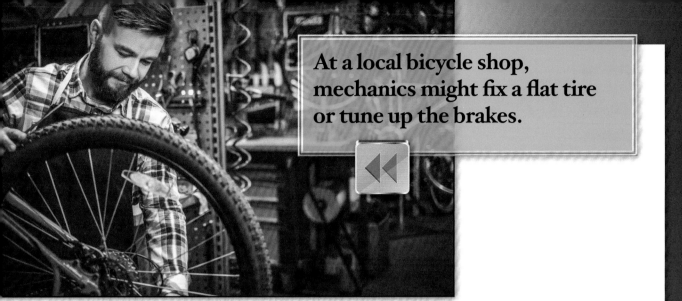

At a local bicycle shop, mechanics might fix a flat tire or tune up the brakes.

is loaded onto large trucks and shipped to supermarkets far away.

Communities usually offer plenty of transportation services. Citizens fill their gas tanks at gas stations and have their vehicles repaired at service stations. Bicycle shops sell and repair bikes. To travel long distances, people board airplanes at their nearest airport.

COMPARE AND CONTRAST

Trains, cars, buses, and bikes are used to get around in communities. What are some of the benefits and drawbacks of each mode of transportation?

Staying in Touch

Imagine receiving a postcard or package in the mail, answering a telephone call, sending a text message, or writing an email. All day long, people send and receive messages. Communication can be fun, like getting a birthday present in the mail. Communication can be important, like telling a parent what time soccer practice is over. And communication can be alarming, like calling 911 for someone who has been in an accident or is hurt.

Many community businesses and services help people communicate.

Some communication still takes place through the mail, such as sending a package.

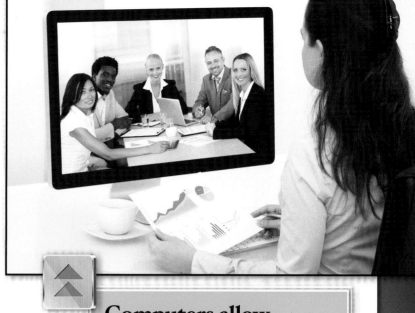

At the post office, people mail letters and packages. Mail can be sent almost anywhere in the world. The telecommunications industry allows citizens to communicate in different ways. Many people use traditional telephones in their homes and carry a cell phone or smartphone to stay in touch wherever they go. The internet makes it possible for people around the world to communicate through computers.

Computers allow businesspeople to communicate over long distances.

THINK ABOUT IT
When should someone use emergency 911 telephone service?

Are You Hungry?

People in different communities have different ways of finding food. In rural communities, people often live on farms and grow their own food. In cities, people shop for food at grocery stores, supermarkets, and local farmers' markets. City dwellers may also choose to eat out at restaurants. They may have a favorite restaurant in their community.

Families enjoy eating out together at their favorite restaurants in their communities.

Some community members grow their own food. Farmers also grow and ship food to local markets or groceries.

The farmers that grow crops and raise animals are providing a service. When food or crops are ready, farmers ship them to markets and to restaurants. If the market is nearby, a farmer's products arrive by truck. If the market is far away, products are transported by truck, train, or ship. The people who do the shipping and run the markets and restaurants also provide a service.

COMPARE AND CONTRAST

What kinds of foods can you find at the grocery store and the farmers' market? How are farmers' market items different?

LET'S HAVE FUN

Communities offer different kinds of places for fun activities. Many friends and families enjoy the outdoors. They hike the trails at a neighborhood park or swim and splash in the pool. Some climb and swing at the playground. They slide down snowy hills or skate across smooth ice. Many parks also sell tasty treats.

Other people might prefer indoor fun. They can watch a movie at the theater or play electronic games at a video arcade. Some like to roll a strike at the

In some places, winters are cold and snowy. Boys and girls play outside and ski, skate, or snowshoe.

Bowling is an indoor sport. Children join their families and friends at the bowling alley for fun.

bowling alley or shoot baskets at an indoor gym or community center.

Community members can choose what they do for fun. Whatever choice they make, there are many places in the community where friends and families can have fun together!

THINK ABOUT IT

Why do you think it's important for communities to have parks?

Looking Your Best

When people get ready for work or school, they usually try to look their best. They do this by getting their hair styled or by wearing nice clothes. There are many different kinds of stores that help people look good.

Hair salons, barbershops, clothing stores, shoe stores, and eyeglass stores are found in many communities. Larger communities have many stores. They have huge shopping malls where consumers purchase many

Salespeople help boys and girls find eyeglasses at optical stores.

In many communities, people have lots of choices when they need to get a haircut.

different kinds of goods and services in one place. Smaller communities usually have fewer stores to provide the citizens' needs and wants.

In communities where several stores sell the same goods or provide the same services, producers must compete for customers. This competition has several results. Consumers receive better service, product quality is improved, and prices are lower for goods and services.

Vocabulary

Competition is the effort of persons or firms to attract business by offering customers the best deal for their goods or services.

Community Services, Past and Future

Communities and their services have changed over time and will continue to change. Years ago, before cars and major highways, communities depended on horses. People rode horses and used them for farm work. Stage coaches transported people and goods using horses.

The wide use of horses meant that there used to be special workers and services for horses and the people who used them. For example,

Nowadays, people ride horses mainly for enjoyment. Long ago, horses were used for transportation and farm work.

Libraries offer a variety of services, such as computer or tablet rentals, job hunting, or help with homework.

blacksmiths made and repaired equipment used for horses and horse travel. Today, people still ride horses, but the services to support them are not as necessary.

THINK ABOUT IT

What new services do you think communities will provide in the future?

Other services have changed as well. Public libraries, for instance, offer more services than just borrowing books. Libraries now provide computer and tablet rentals, online resources, and help for people seeking jobs.

Community services are available wherever people live, work, and play. Citizens, neighborhoods, and communities succeed because of community services.

GLOSSARY

blueprint A photographic print made with white lines on a blue background and used especially for copying mechanical drawings, maps, and architects' plans.

compete To strive for something.

consumer A person who buys and uses goods and services.

deposit To put money in a bank.

goods Manufactured articles or products of art or craft.

industry The businesses that provide a particular product or service.

loan Money lent at interest.

market A meeting together of people to buy and sell.

pollute To spoil (as a natural resource) with waste made by humans.

producer A person who grows agricultural products or manufactures articles.

recycling Reusing materials instead of throwing them away.

rural Of or relating to the country, country people or life, or agriculture.

services Useful labor that does not produce goods.

supermarket A market selling foods and household items.

telecommunications Communication that takes place across a distance.

transportation Method of moving from one place to another.

urban Related to or typical of being in a city.

For More Information

Books

Andrews, Carolyn. *What Are Goods and Services?* New York, NY: Crabtree Publishing Company, 2008.

Capici, Gaetano. *How Did That Get to My House? Mail.* North Mankato, MN: Cherry Lake Publishing, 2009.

Kalman, Bobbie. *Places in My Community.* New York, NY: Crabtree Publishing Company, 2010.

Kreisman, Rachelle. *Places We Go: A Kids' Guide to Community Buildings.* South Egremont, MA: Red Chair Press, 2015.

Masters, Nancy R. *How Did That Get to My House? Water.* North Mankato, MN: Cherry Lake Publishing, 2010.

Ritchie, Scot. *Look Where We Live! A First Book of Community Building.* Toronto, ON: Kids Can Press, 2015.

Websites

Because of the changing nature of internet links, Rosen Publishing has developed an online list of websites related to the subject of this book. This site is updated regularly. Please use this link to access the list:

http://www.rosenlinks.com/LFO/services

INDEX